TRULY PERTINENT QUESTIONS

TRULY
PERTINENT
QUESTIONS

BY

WAYNE D. RUSSELL

ARPress
ILLUMINATING IDEAS
EMPOWERING VOICES

ARPress
45 Dan Road Suite 5
Canton MA 02021

Hotline: 1(888) 821-0229
Fax: 1(508) 545-7580

Ordering Information:
Quantity sales.Special discounts are available on quantity purchases by corporations, associations, and others.For details, contact the publisher at the address above.

Printed in the United States of America.

ISBN-13:   Paperback   979-8-89356-606-2
             eBook   979-8-89356-607-9

Library of Congress Control Number: 2024903453

Table Of Contents

PREFACE

Truly Pertinent Questions is a is an anthology of poems that occupy the mind of an eclectic Jamaican living in the metropolis called New York City. This compilation contains the story of a soldier, an educator, an intellectual, and an activist who he examines salient questions that are in his heart and on his mind. These poems and songs are his attempt to illuminate the existential and, more so, the transcendental.

Russell's work explores the quantum realm. It is best described as a fusion of the radical lyrical overtones of Robert Nesta 'Bob' Marley, coupled with the philosophical undertones of Marcus Mosiah Garvey and infused with traces of the intellect and sophistication of Prof. Rex Nettleford. In short, his work is a passionate ethnic blend that appeals to all the senses.

FORWARD

Russell's work takes the talented through theatrical enclaves. The vibrations from drums radiating rhythmic signals, chants and calculated movements place one in a conscious time and space domain. This work is a contribution to the world's populace. Medgar Evers College and Polytechnic University have once again enriched the world

Dr. JJ Kwame Nutakor

DEDICATION

Somewhere - nestled in the hills of St. Elizabeth, west of Holland Bamboo and north of YS Falls, lies Springfield. Here the cool breeze dances with the clouds and the morning sun wrestles through a light pink mist to kiss cascading peaks that seem to sleep at the feet of God. As faith should have it, we are not at that place

Thanks to Joy, Ruth, Yvonne, Jhoanne, Regina, and Risa for years of critique and encouragement

The hills, they ripple across the backbone of my native land in descending hues of faded blues and emerald greens…I see them now within dreams. The streets of Brooklyn must now suffice as my domestic paradise

For there is a garden in full bloom in the quantum realm. It is where high Theta resides, and Epsilon portends, and it gently flows through the tip of my pen. Thanks you Mom (Edna Alberta Russell), thanks Dad (Ismael Author Russell); for the love that you gave, and it still flow now from yonder graves. It was written before it was truly understood; and all done for the greater good.

...Regarding Purpose

NKYINKYIM

I authored poems before words were ever spoken
Morphed into serpents before promises were broken
Never for one moment should you doubt my abilities
I am the architect of time and the purveyor of *VERSATILITY*.

PURPOSE

(List poem—content)

MY PURPOSE [*is simple*]
THESE WORDS [*may hurt*]
I AM THE POET [*I am blessed and cursed; I seek no fame*]
I WRITE TO SCARE THE PAIN AWAY [*it's unabridged, I know you thirst for...*]
THE TRUTH ABOUT THE METAVERSE [*For what it's worth we are not the first*]

MY PURPOSE

What is my purpose?
I preserve reality…
by massaging words into verses.

THESE WORDS

This is a poem from the heart
And long after the time it will still exist
It speaks of love, of joy
and the birth of emotion
It takes ocean of thoughts
and sets them in motion
These words will spark insurrections and eternal rage
Each and every line, every single page
Whether chanted from pulpits or uttered from stage.

These words will open doors
won't be underscored
and will prove that after the end –
there is still much more
And as faith burns in fire and man lose sight
They will breed hope in the depth of our night
And within that said darkness they will spark a light
These words will enlighten offenders, flush out pretenders
Cause dreamers to dream dreams and cause fears to surrender.

These words will be followed
these words are not hallowed
They will prove love is sacred
and hatred is shallow
And if love lives these words will be on man's mind,
they speak of dreams unborn and the cyclic nature of time
They bellow, love is a cradle and is eternally mine
These words were truly conceived by the hopes and achieves
Of those who have had visions and who dared to believe.

And as west winds drifts into extinguishing star
These words will be uttered both near and far
And if promises are broken
Faith is a token
Souls will sink to their knees
and these words will be spoken
These words will be spoken.
These Words - These Words
This…is a poem - from the Heart.

I AM THE POET

I am the poet…living in my own time
Creating my own rhymes
Moving to my rhythm with the flicker of a pen

I am the creator of happy endings.
I can send tears to your cheeks
Why? You ask
Why…because I've seen through the eyes of my soul
I've felt our fathers' anguish, their slaughter
The loss of ten thousand dreams
But as hope shatters - while you sleep - I write my piece
For I'm the historian, watching my ancestral track
Calculating the bearing, recording the drift.
I am the poet

I am the poet
The man who begs for your understanding
It's a cruel world but in all its adversities - I smile
For as I die, I've written on paper
Words that will outlive my flesh
And in the same breath - set my soul free…
I am the poet.

I WRITE TO SCARE THE PAIN AWAY

I love you - for there's just no other way
So, there are restless nights and quiet days
So as mortals kneel, and while sinners pray -
I write…to take the pain away.
As much as joy - knows no sorrow
I love you like there's no tomorrow
So, tears form puddles where voiceless children play
There are no shelters here, the rains…they stay -
I write - to take the pain away.
Only the lonely - knows loneliness
I love you without conditions or pretexts
With pure resolutions—void of context
And there are sacred verses I dare not say -
So, I write…to scare the pain away.
I love you and I am afraid…
I am afraid - that you are afraid
That you will see your fears - in me
That you have forgotten what all those glorious moments meant
That you have surrendered your hopes and the dreams you dreamt
That you have forgotten the yesterdays we, lost souls, spent
For we never laid naked on canvas and made love for all of humanity
Never painted a masterpiece of joy, and basked at the brink of insanity
I fear that in this morbid dismal world - our skies will forever be gray
So, I write this poem of love, hope and devotion - to scare the pain away.

THE TRUTH ABOUT THE METAVERSE

The questions that will forever reverberate

Are not those found in hyperspace.

They are the questions that are unrehearsed

And have no conception of the metaverse.

These questions speak of love, of telos, and of a requiem

That will soothe our souls as we face our end.

These are not questions that are beyond our grasp

They are not in vogue...so, they are seldom asked.

So, I am not here by chance, in fact, it is my sole intention

To ask these truly pertinent questions.

...Regarding Love

OSRAM NE NSOROMMA

And what of my origins?
I will tell you as it was told to me
Without any flairs or pleasantries
I am the soot of extinguishing stars in regal conformity
So, I resonate in vibrating strings in pure celestial *HARMONY.*

LOVE

(List poem - content)

LOVING YOU [*makes me*]
COMPLETE [*I may*]
REQUEST [*that you stay here with me*]
THIS POEM [*creates*]
A PLACE [*it lives right here on this page. It rages*]
LIKE FIRE [*and offers us a space. See,*]
I AM ME [*in truth, I am just longing to be free. To say*]
HELLO [*or get close to you. My love is*]
PRECIOUS AND TRUE [*and meant for you. So.*]
CHEERS [*my love, this might sound surreal*]
REMEMBER ME [*if by chance you become*]
UNBOUNDED [*for we truly never know. We might be like those White*]
ORCHIDS IN THE SNOW

My love for the moment we dance free.

LOVING YOU

For those who are yet to bear witness will have to question
The sincerity of my thoughts and the depth of my affection
For I sprinkle starlight and snowflakes and place them above
So, I can light up your darkness and shower you with love.
My love is as ancient as Ma'at
Forgoing lakes – splitting mountains
Tumbling hard water from Quasars
to form celestial fountains
My love - my love!
How much do I love thee?
How much!
Loving you is like the breath that I take
Effortless, natural and without mistake
Loving you is like Galaxies in their awakening
Filling eternity with songs, leaving me breathless and shaken.
Loving you is like glory – leaving the heavens all bright
Desecrate the darkness, filling my soul with light
My love is all encompassing my love is complete
As God is my witness, I place these words at your feet.
My love…my love
How much do I love you…I dare not say!

COMPLETE

What If my incompleteness is purely by design?
And I can see the missing pieces deep in your eyes.
Tonight, my thoughts are on you
Tonight, my thoughts are pure
And sometimes we face the world, and we feel so insecure
Remember there's no load too heavy
For I'll be there to help you bear
And in those apprehensive moments
I'll let you know how much I care.
Faith has led me to you
And the rocky path that often brings us pain
Is sometimes the very gate that leads us to brighter days
For there is a land somewhere in the back of my mind
And I can close my eyes and see it oh so clearly sometimes
I believe that all things have their season, everything - its place
I've found completeness for I close my eyes and see your face.

What if my incompleteness is by design?
And my notion of God and eternity is locked in your smile.
Tonight, my thoughts are of you
Thoughts of quiet nights, star-lit skies
Of all I've ever wanted and what is unmistakably mine
Of souls surrendering to a force much greater than them
Of all that is great and small and things we're yet to comprehend.
For I do believe… and I know this to be true
I find completeness when I'm looking at you.

REQUESTS

"With the greatest of certainty as you swear from your heart
In those very same instant things start falling apart."

'Do not question me, for I know no answer!'
Just that I crave your every being
You will always be my sobering thought
That shakes my soul with truth and reason
The gentle touch of descending dew, angel's wings
and…all kinds of secret special things.

'Do not wake me for I know no rest!'
We did not lose each other we just ascended to a higher plane
To greater heights and outside of the rain
Where pain drives poets to write sonnets and villanelles
Where thinkers unravel life and demystify hell.

'Do not touch me lest I sin'
I do not need to understand for there're things I can't refute
And in all this chaos and turmoil, I only seek to know the truth
I am hollow without frame standing here without pretext
And in this my final hour I'm simply making these requests.

THIS POEM

This is a poem to the unhappy
Those who have discovered love
after it had slipped through their fingers - shattered
and waited too long to pick up the pieces

This is a poem to the lonely
who let go of a dream to chase a butterfly
which has a dream to find a flower in a garden,
in a dream that sees not its grace.

This is a poem to the weak
who released love
when the weight, the stress, and the pain
tested their sincerity
when the pressure of fellowship
bared its strain upon them.

This is a poem to the faithless
those who failed to soothe the pain.
Who failed to embrace a lonely soul
and are now the victims out of control
In a happy crowd, but very much…alone.

A PLACE

There is a place
There is a place.
There is a place for lonely souls
Where very few will dare to go
Where it is safe for me to cry
To cast away my foolish pride
And there I don't have to be that strong
For it is safe to say I'm wrong.

It's just a secret special place
Where to each, there is a space
A void, a vacuum that's hard to find
And there my troubles I can hide
When I'm confused it's there, I stand…
to try to better to understand.

So, if by chance I take you there
It shows how very much I care
To share a moment…to let love grow
I think it's fair - you ought to know!
Dreams are forever - pure and true
A magic dream led me to you.

So…in my special place I stand
I'm all alone with pen in hand
I'm painting rainbows in the sky
A star…no two - a nursery rhyme
A chart to guide all lonely souls
Out of this void…that I call home,
There is a place.
There is a place.

LIKE FIRE

Like fire. Like thunder. Like rain.

Like fire...
desire comes to life
in the silence of a heartbeat.
Now weary eyes know no rest
For you rage in my heart, on my mind.
Every breath rings melody of a place unseen but sensed.
Of passion unknown yet felt
As the foreverness of time slips like sand through an hour-glass
Ending too soon, revealing hidden chambers
In places long forgotten, creating worlds in a teardrop.

Like thunder...
Souls roar in ecstasy
In the canyon of a mind struggling to define your grace
I grow weak, too weak to care, too strong to forget
Too ready to embrace this emptiness
Growing weary at the futility of a love unborn
A fragile heart lies shivering -
At the anticipation of a... touch.

Like rain...
Iron bars encase a soul
Imprisoned by despair anchored to the darkness.
Faded memories of smiles...of words,
of strangers sharing secrets in the dark.
Leaves me crying, leaves me forever reaching out to...
Can you hear me souls of opposing stars?
In a universe too wide for wishes to be heard
Too vast for dreamers to dream
Too barren for hope to grow
Can you hear me ...can you hear me?
Like fire, like thunder, like rain
Like fire, like thunder, like rain.

I AM ME

They told me…
If I straightened my hair -
I would look better.
If my face was narrow -
I would get the part.
If I had thin lips -
I would make it.
If my eyes were blue -
I would be pretty.
If I were fairer -
Life would be easy.

But I am not you.
In your eyes - I will not look better.
I will never play the part.
I will not make it in your society -
For I am not beautiful in your sight
And - it has not been easy.

My hair is course - lush,
It traps my soul within my body
My face is as wide as my mother's -
Like her mother - beautiful.
My lips are thick – full–they symbolize:
Prudence,
Affection,
Passion.
Mine eyes are as black as Midnight's Sun.
My skin...**NOT BLACK ENOUGH!**
And true - Life has been hard.

HELLO

Hello…
The world will never know your name
But you are the fabric of dreams
You're the forbidden fruit that eludes me
You will remain…nameless
You are the force that guides me
the reason great men write poems and songs
that change humanity
For those songs and poems shall force lesser men to
find greater truth
And truth shall lead them to questions
And questions, to answers…or the lack thereof
And unanswered questions will breed dissention
And from the womb of dissention comes anarchy
And anarchy will breed revolutionaries
And revolutionaries - they will march
Because of a void that exists within their hearts
Because they have yet to see your eyes
Or feel the warmth of your embrace
So, they will swing their swords in your honor,
In your name - a name they know not
And they will fall
And they will die
And others shall hear of their death
And they too will raise Cain upon humanity
And nations will plunge into wars and sink into chaos
Because I never heard your voice at the break of dawn
Because I never tasted your lips on a moon-lit night
Because we never ran naked in the summer breeze
Because you never stood close enough - to me.

PRECIOUS AND TRUE

For all that is sacred and true and cherished
Above all other things
are the thoughts that dwell deep within
that rests upon minds on quiet evenings
and in silent moments - token of our past.
For darkness knows - no tears
nor is it swayed by secrets kept.
Without reason passion emerges from our emptiness
And lays prey upon unsuspecting souls
And scribes will write and thinkers - ponder
And searchers of truth will remain sleepless
For rest comes with answers
And there are none - there are none.

For all that is sacred, true, and cherished
And seldom spoken of but taken to grave
I reveal now
But never again shall these things part from my lips,
Nor shall it be written of, or made reference to:
I love you hopelessly
Without reason
Without apologies
Without question
Without notion of time
Or sense of responsibility
Without pride
Without mercy
I surrender my silence but for a moment
For all that is sacred precious and true...
I say no more.

CHEERS

Cheers to happiness
- and those who know her well
Cheers to understanding
- and those who will live to tell
Cheers to hope and magic dreams and silly things we do
Cheers to all the simple things, the many and the few.

Cheers to new beginnings
- and the will to start again
Cheers to determinations
- I hope to see you at the end.
Cheers to dreams and aspirations - the hope of things to come
For even in our darkest night, we'll rise to see the sun.

Cheers to strength of spirit
- to stand amid the thorn.
Cheers for wishful thinking
- it is here great dreams are born
Cheers to doubts and uncertainties it shows that we have grown
To accept that there are many things - we'll never really know.

REMEMBER ME

Sometimes…In the darkness
I whisper your name – softly.
I clasp the universe in my hands
And kiss you as you sleep with the air that I breathe.
I trap pulses from extinguishing stars
To form a halo around your soul
So, in my absence - you're not alone.
I am more than I appear to be
I exist in dreams so you can command me
I am here in the emptiness- I'm the seen and unseen
And in the absence of air - in your presence I breathe.
Roses are the manifestation of love and desire
They form silk like petals that showers glory like fire.
I sprinkle silver snowflakes upon your nakedness
You shiver in silence as I kiss your breast.
But with you in my heart I can give nothing less
So, I've created worlds in your likeness
I have erected obelisks in your name
I've propelled energy particles into higher planes
God, Lord, Man, and Father I am one in the same.
I have loved you before - don't you remember me?
It was I who summoned Mars into Aquarius
Pounded giant asteroids into interstellar dust
Built the sphinx in your image because it was just
If your God is within me, then whom can you trust?
I've harnessed energy from Quasars to form celestial patterns
Wrapped them and forged them to form rings around Saturn.
My love will exist in the abyss of time
This love will be encrypted on archeological finds
And these words will forever rage on your mind
For in your nights and in your days, I'll be next to thee
And as long as there's breath you will remember me.

UNBOUNDED

Don't be afraid of things that are hidden
Or try to rationalize the things that are given
Only those who wish to see beyond the facade of reality
Are driven to interpret and simultaneously ignore its fallacies
Is their uniqueness in this realm, is there even humanity?
The question bears more significance than its answer
There are those who can see rapture at the onset of its birth
They embrace doubts for they are certain they will figure it out
That ordinate desire to find symmetry in this enormity of space.
For surely, there is uncertainty in the things that we must face.
The unpredictability of expectations, increased permeation
The totality of The Present without its carnal adoration
Let us envision the glory locked within our emptiness
We are boundaries and defined by the iridescence lights within
Confined by conjecture —we extracted from our ghastly nights
To understand the nature of the Cosmos we need not look above
For, what if all of humanity is woven in serenity and love?
Is it our resolve to realize it, or at least, embrace its ubiquity?
What if we in its deconstruction there is a celestial simplicity?
See - to know is just to recognize that greater unknown exists
Is there more than a golden garden at the end of the Abyss?
So, some will find wisdom and solace in a kiss
love brings vitality and cohesion, if one dare to persist.
Answers are often overrated intrusions that elicit the opposite
Let it be known that ruptured souls have no quest for adoration
They lack the ionized particles that yield glorified sensation
Eliciting elation, exaltation leaving souls excited and wet.
It conjures the shaking of loins and leaves the heart palpitating
Soul versus soul, new dimensionless look what love has created
'Ask me once more if love exists!'
It's the very air we breathe the fabric of dreams
the very force that lured you here - to me.

ORCHIDS IN THE SNOW

So, the end is the beginning –so another day has come
Leaves my fingers slowly tapping—to the beat of distant drums
For I 've been given more than most, so...If humanity should cry
I'd pen a simple song of hope - to dry her weeping eyes.

For there's a choir - they are singing ...a cantata without words
To an audience that is listening, to a silence never heard
I'm strong enough to stand up - if the walls around me fall
And still script the muted voices, of the children down the hall

Moments, they 're yours to treasure; so, take the time to play
Feed the child that lives within you, soon our memories will fade
All that is left of our inactions are floating ashes left in our wake
And the pendulum keeps swinging, stealing time we can't replace.

If he loves you, as I love you — he will know what you are worth
I pray the universe has blessed you, with the love that you deserve
You know— I love you for all seasons ...the way that warrior poets do
I love you in rhymes and verses — and, you know, that much is true.

Call on me when you get lonely, and I will come to lend a hand
I've etched my soul in coded verses, in ways you'll come to understand
See, the gentle fear you have of me -- will, one day, slowly dissipate
And a gentle wind will kiss a mist upon your wrinkled face.

And on one dreary winter's night —-the world will come to know
The reason why I could not speak the truth of which I've been told
For, the end is the beginning - so...I come here to write again
True love is forever fluid – raining teardrops from my pen
You should love him, for he is gentle - still there is one thing you should
know
See...the angels never left us – they 're just white Orchids in the snow.

...Regarding Revolutionary Paradigms

AKOBEN

With sword in hand, I come to pray
I ask for a place for our kids to play
I pray they'd come to understand
That in every single circumstance
To seek faith, compassion, and *VIGILANCE.*

PARADIGMS

(List poem)

I AM [*the*]
WORDS [*at the edge of*]
INFINITY [*spewing*]
THE SEED [*of dissention. Giving birth to*]
STRING THEORY [*I am*]
THE EYES OF HERU [*Sky and Sun so, I come, indivisible. I am the*]
ONE [*I saw the viper in the grassy knolls. Watched the dreaded*]
THE SCHEME [*concocted, and exposed...*]
AFTER THE PARADE [*will not be permitted to call me by*]
MY NAME.

I spew at the edge of divisible dreams...as the darkness that you see.

I AM

I am, I am, I am.
I am all things, and nothing - yet shaper of dreams.
The line that divides the seen and unseen.
And the vastness in time is the oneness in me -
I'm the Surveyor of Truth - Suspender of Galaxies.
I'm like the substance in the ether -
I permeate time...shuffling stars into astrological signs.
For the past, the present and future that's me
dispelling your pseudo- Greek mythology.
For I span Infinity like infinity is one
I'm the erector of the Zenith house of the Sun-
I am the everlasting light - The Trinity.
The God, the Father, The Negro - all three.
The vision of light in the darkness - I am
Powers that rage in the silence - I am
Glory that shines in the blackness - I am
For I am! Yes...I am.

For I am darkness the absence of light
celestial energy the brilliance of night.
I am the cradle of civilization
The voice of a Nation
The Alpha, The Omega The beginning and ...again
Again, I am – you...me...thee
fountains of power, uncharted sea
for, all of the untold mysteries
are watered-down conversions of-- mystical me.
Conjured ethnic chants, cosmic mystical rhymes
swaying to an ensemble of celestial vibes
bursting with energies, transcending all times
spinning the fluid of life - with a hype.
I am a vision of tomorrow dread of today, Ill-fated yesterday
I am your salvation, to God - ME - we pray.
I am the reminder of injustice, the root of all ills
The servant before you, the power within -
The Superego, the ego, and the id
The builder of pyramids, the true giver of life
I am the proverbial symbol of darkness in light
For I am, I am! I ... am!

WORDS

Words don't come easy anymore.
Whisper - echoes in the emptiness
Voices - float in the darkness
Trying to shuffle thoughts into stacks
to somehow make sense of reality
Trying to see your eyes
Trying to touch your soul
Trying to say ...I don't know
Words don't come easy anymore.
Smiles fade in our silence
Dreams flutter like gulls that float
upon tides, near - but too far to touch
Wish there were time to sing
TO carve castle in the sand
Wish we could run - Wish we could cry
Wish we could say...
Words don't come easy anymore.
Now there is laughter
Unspoken words swirl in the canyon of a mind
Fading echoes, sealed lips, lost dreams
Now tears are the residue of our silence
Standing in the puddle of the tears we cry
are souls that have forgotten how to fly
How to sing - How to sigh - How to wh-is-per
Words don't come easy anymore.

INFINITY

[Infinities are contorted zeros]

There are no Black holes, just - gateways to eternity
Am I the creator of my uncertainty?
Sometimes the search beyond is the search within.
Horus and Osirus hmm...let us begin:

I ...
I am not of this time.
I exhale and create galaxies
while my children... blow Nebulas from drinking straws
And you don't know who I am?
From out of darkness, I came - Light.
Yes, it was I who unraveled time
That pseudo-continuum of twisted and broken lines
I am the intrusion that shines

I exist in the innermost and outermost boundaries
At rest, I am the midpoint of adjoining points
In motion I am that which lies at the convergence of dimensions
Void of space void of time
I am conversely at rest, stationary
Sojourning - between adjoining points...zero
I am everything - I am nothing...I am infinity.
[Do not re-read less, you lose the essence]

THE SEED

The hidden seed
has grown
In the darkness
beneath the Rose
Beneath...the Rose you cherished.
I bow
in silence
Rose so fair
for only you can bring my tears.
But in your folly
failed to see.
Beneath the earth
my roots run free
This lifeless shrub
This useless plant
could one day cause an avalanche.
The Rose that you have cultured – true...
You pull me up - The Rose dies too.

STRING THEORY

Zweng!!! Zweng!!! Zweng!!! Zweng!!! (Vibrating strings)
Quarks are sparks generated between black lips
As they kiss to eclipse the Sun.
Sending '*colors*' and '*flavor*', we savor in cosmic rays
I block hostilities, for they create a mess and at best
They stain the sanctum of my holiness - so I stand correct
for I must attest to a duality of which I am certain
I claim, God and man are one in person
So reverently, I come to thee
I hum to free myself from gravity
For insanity prevents my hair to lock
So I block lepton shocks as they fall from the sky
They are asking' me why?
But I just sigh open my third eye
and create explosions in the ocean
causing electromagnetic motion
to change the '*spins*' on sub-atomic particles
So, rewrite your articles
They were also wrong about photons
I know their energies and positions
In fact, they have one salient mission
To rise to a higher energy state and give greater emission
There are no admissions to these facts; somebody say: '*word!*'
They claim that time is linear, but that notion is absurd
It is cycles that regulate the earth
It is cycloids and spirals that inundate the Universe
There is chaos in order and so too is the reverse
The dances of Nature are surely unrehearsed
But I am cursed, enshrouded, trapped in this flesh that I wear...but
I have gone past the bitterness, gone past the tears.
Black souls don't roam we exist between time zones
We fill dark places occupy spaces between dilated time -
Lines are constricted at the speed of light
And are bent around great masses of gasses that we call stars
Seen from projects and through prison bars
So I illuminate dark matter to foster the creation
For color precedes words and antecedes civilization
I clench my black fist to signal a Nation
To move creation with the power of the minds

For we were enslaved before for being too kind
Now I've plotted the path of galaxies on their proverbial spin
And found that the darkness in space is the darkness within
And light is the illusion that causes man to sin
So I begin so I end I'm neither foe nor friend
I vibrate strings at higher frequencies to start life again.
Zweng!!! Zweng!!! Zweng!!! Zweng!!!

THE EYES OF HERU

...I am he who dwells in his Eye, I have come that I may give Maat to Re, I have propitiated Seth with the bodily fluids of Aker and the blood which is in the spinal cord of Geb.'

Do you
remember me my love?
My woman is like blue

Graceful	as the sky
As tranquil	as the sea and
Yet she is	anchored
To this	dim reality
I am	Amen
I exist	in dreams
and roar	in the
sounds of	drums as
It beats	In your sleep
And as I	speak

In the   tongue
of your mother I can
feel your essence
My Woman is blue
I must rest
A full three days
Before I ascend to the upper chambers—come! —walk with me
Let me tell you your purpose here and you can tell me mine
Let me tell you why we no longer fly let me kiss you as I did
then, under the thirteenth moons that blessed our purple sky
Let me tell you why
you cry here
here on Earth
This is not the
Place of your birth
My woman in blue
My love in blue yet to
Be understood by those
Mortals who seek to define
You with words they are yet to
Understand that you exist in symbols.

ONE

(Form poem)

Am I
alone?
I scan
the darkness.
"Is there
anyone
out here
anyone
in here?
No just
you me.
Just us
we. Just
me. Just
us? No – one!

THE SCHEME

Feel the texture of my World
Rigid, jagged…perfectly - imperfect
Like these lace dungeon walls
Your Liberty imprisons me
The juxtaposed notion of I and we
Leaves me bleeding like -
your eroded concept of individuality
Confined in the cubicle designed for me defined by thee
I exist therein, and whilst there - '*I am free*'
In this- my space- I create my reality
Within the space, you've given me
to fit existing specifications.
Ostensible free to lead my nation
to the light of your salvation -'*If you will me*'
In the darkness of my soul
I've concocted happiness
From the radioactive lies, you gave to me
I've been shaped by your imagery
Now my son will see my creativity
Through the eyes of your Prism
And those who shout praises to thee
Will be honored and renowned through eternity
See - I am no longer me…
I am a product of acclimation - an assimilated mutt
Who has learned to distrust - to keep my mouth shut.
to swallow my pride – '*Keeps ya eyes on da prize!*'
And despite the agitation, there is no collective dream
Just one salient theme:
The Neo-Colonial schemes
So, Utopia for you, ain't…Utopia for me.
Here…feel the texture of my dream.

AFTER THE PARADE

Who will sing a song after the curtain closes?
After the fanfare - after the parade
They won't see me cry
Nor quiver in fear
My sadness…My sadness I'll bear
It is the moment of happiness that I fear
I fear wanting - like I've been wanting you
Loving - like I've loved you
The anticipation of a familiar touch
…Your touch

They won't see me cry
Stoop down in knee-deep self-pity
Nor shivering in recluse
My sadness…My sadness I'll bear
I will be the fool singing in the rain
Smiling for the tears simply trickle inside
They won't see me cry

Who will march after the battle?
But those who have no home
Those who fail to find solace in the sublime
Those who cannot find time

They won't see me cry
Nor shall I find religion
And pray for forgiveness or salvation
I simply dry these tears from my wretched eyes
For they won't see me cry.

MY NAME

All I have are words...

I write for those who have forgotten the splendor of life's moments,
For thoughts that never took flight because of words never spoken
I write for the unrealized longing, for the fragility of time
For the not-so-transitory acts that leave stains upon man's mind
I capture images in obscure sentences to capture questionable truth
And adorn them with rhythmic schemes that render them pure and absolute
I drafted insidious devious verses to trap vile and abhorrent sensations
Then titillating quiescence passion in fiery couplets only moments later
I shook lines from descending souls on one cold and bitter evening
And deconstructed them into stanzas giving them new angelic meanings
I crafted sonnets for warring factions, and it did quell their derision
Stacked iambic pentametric arrangements that gave the ignoble vision
I have tried giving hope to the anguished and respite to the disdained...
The ode I sent the dammed was coded...now they know me by my name
I am cold and defiance and will die only when my work is done
And my Epitaph will scream resistance causing other sentinels to come.

...Regarding Space and Time

NKYIMU

I am structurally composed as my tradition dictates

Builders of pyramids, charter of stars I do proclaim

Aberrant, yet symmetric I've made it my mission

To be detailed, absolute, and exact in my *PRECISION*.

SPACE'S TIMELINE

(List poem)

EMPTY... [*as*]
TIME [*formless*]
INTERMEDIATE [*in this*]
SPACE [*filled with the*]
SOUNDS OF BLACKNESS [*I speak of*]
DARK MATTER [*filled with*]
QUESTIONS [*formless*]
THE EMPTY HOUSE [*is my universe*]
WHAT'S THE POINT? [*...of my existence*]

Is my universe formless – or is it filled with my Emptiness?

EMPTY
(Form poem)

There is this emptiness inside of me, a hollow, void, a shallow wavering low gray mist that lives here within me. It surrounds

my soul	my soul
And it's	hurting.
And there	… are no
no words	to make
amends	loneliness
has been	my only
friend she	reminds
me of the	simple little
things.	There is
a lingering	unnerving
sensation	gnawing
at me sending	shockwaves
in my room our	this room
room Where	we once
lay.	There is
so much	space in
abyss of	unadulterated
emptiness	just pure
Nothingness	and I cannot

tell nor dare deny the true depth of my unsanctioned sacrifice but despite all my pleasantry and this insidious smile, there is a little bit of this emptiness trapped in these eyes. A little bit of this emptiness - just a bit of this emptiness making me cry.

TIME

A series of related events
Time determines action
Inasmuch as action needs time to determine posture.
Action and time are ignobly entangled.

INDETERMINATE

Remember...all hyperspace curves are straight lines.
Truth is the observer's perception of reality

Can you see me?
Have you ever closed your eyes and seen the universe?
Expanding and children shouting yeahhh!
Can you hear my voice - their voices?
Listen hard and you will see them
You will see them playing in familiar places
Look at their faces and you will find
That they are the faces from your past
Faces from you dreams
Dancing upon a page as you lay in bed
Dancing on your walls, playing in your head.

This statement begs the question
The question of reality and universal purpose
There may be various states of uniqueness
This ruptures the notion of singularity
Therefore, there can be no prime objective
Humanity could coalesce in a single higher order being
Converge into one collective consciousness
So we could be one entity and the God force we seek
Could it be here within me?

Can you see me?
Can you here my voice?
Can you hear my voice within you?
Dancing in an expanding Universe
While the kids playing shouting yeah.
Kids with familiar faces.
Listen hard – Can you determine what is real.

SPACE

One's field of dream, the sphere of one's influence
Coupled with the perturbations that emanate from my existence.
It is my realm - the medium on which all-observable events are
sketched…along with the consequence of my desire.

SOUND OF BLACKNESS

Sound the abeng!
Rise warrior
Hear the words of the prophets
Four hundred years erode the bondage
Awake Oh spirits of my ancestors
Strike stretched skin great messenger
send your cryptic codes
Ashanti! Cameroon! Shabazz!
dide! dide!
Here's the dawn
The Black Renaissance
Make your stance,
Oh, mighty race - I hear your war cries...
Walking the night
Four-hundred thousand naked feet
striking the ground
causing the Earth to shiver in fear
Opening the eyes of creation
As the soul of man crumbles:
To the sounds of - **BLACKNESS.**

DARK MATTER

The fabric of space that is old and has lost its luster
It is the non-luminous parts of any star cluster.

QUESTIONS
(Form poem)

In ultimate chaos
what is   serenity?
Is there   singularity?
Is the darkness me
or the essence
of my ungodliness?
What if I am God?
and I'm just basking
in the midst of your
doubt?
Would you
Worship me?
Would you
recognize me?
Clad in a pair of
Nike sneakers,
T-shirt and
an old pair
of blue Jeans.
Christ –would
you know me?
I often think
about these
things.

Gosh!
Tell me
…Is this
blasphemy?

THE EMPTY HOUSE

It was empty
but her walls told a story
as it embraced me
and her corners spoke softly.
Blue personified her sensations
Her floor massaged my feet
Her walls echoed voices
of years gone by playing a familiar
repertoire of laughter…of joy.
I looked to her ceiling - white
and saw visions of a hundred yesterdays.
I was a stranger
but somehow, I felt welcome
"I love you - still", she said was
I alone?
I knew then that I was not
then a warmth enshrouded me
A warmth – I'd never felt before
like spirits from some ancient past
She gently held me in its grasp
I was alone
but not in solitude
I looked to her ceiling
and said, "I love you too."
And then she whispered,
"Welcome home."
…the house is empty now.

WHAT IS THE POINT?

Points are insignificant
Unless they are heralded into arrays
But infinite numbers of points form a ray
When terminated - forms segments of lines
Out of singularity comes time—a continuum
Existing with breath, it starts, and it ends
Continuing if the paper meets pen
For there is no thickness in its entire extent
The single-dimensional set gives rise to the entity - length.

Infinite juxtaposed lines form sheets
Visible from orthogonal position are planes
Accommodating duality appearing the same
From equidistant called center from which
It extends covering area occupying regions
Like swarming crusaders or legionnaires
Line times line, not one, but the pair
Multiplicity, second order quantified by the square.

...Regarding God and the Universe

ADOBE SANTANN

Please lend me your ears – for all you know-
I'm as blessed as I'm cursed
I am the all-seeing eyes the Protector of the 13th
UNIVERSE

PRAYERS

(List poem)

WHAT IF? [*in solitude, I knelt and*]
I PRAY [*to the*]
UNIVERSE [*and while*]
IN THE PRESENCE OF GOD [*She told me that I am*]
THE MESSAGE [*and I said to her- which one? For oftentimes*]
I DREAM [*of God in luminescent*]
SIMPLICITY [*She said: Indeed, it is not I in me you seek*]
THE BEGINNING [*was not marked by affable regality*]
CAN YOU FEEL LOVE [*in its purest form its void of pomposity*]
WARRIOR POETS [*, and sentinels they dosometimes seek clarity*]
INTANGIBLE [*and fragile are the rewards that reap*]
IS IT I [*who rock the cradle so that mortals could go sleep*]
LET IT BE.[*known that I am here beside you constantly*]

They were like floating mist screaming...in their solitude

WHAT IF?

What If
we were children
all young, and gay, and free

What If
we were the mighty wind
That calmed the angry sea

What If
We were only lily buds
In a pond longing to be.

And What If life has greater meaning
beyond our sparse reality
And we are simply butterflies.
Encased within a dream.

I PRAY

My dreams are of today
For each day brings greater uncertainty
I pray for tomorrow: I hope that life will be grateful.

My joy, is within me
For smiles are from the soul
A reflection of the inner man
Whom, I'm yet to understand.

My faith, is in you
For alone I cannot bear
So, help me walk this barren land
And if I should fall... please, help me stand.

My love is yours
You're the fuel that propels me
The reason I go on
So, sing- lift my spirit with your songs.

I hope the dream
I have that one-day faith
Will bring me Joy comes true,
And love – please, guide me through this storm.
For these things, I humbly pray.

THE UNIVERSE

I am a universe beyond tomorrow and a breath away from eternity
I loved you before you understood the shadows
Before you knew what was sacred and hollowed
I need not cloak you – need not bask in your presence
For I am past and present tense I was sent...
I am the essence of time spent unfolding unscripted verses
I need not speak for I scream in your silence
Dear not write for I echo in your emptiness
I know who you are ---

IN THE PRESENCE OF GOD

Is it, at all, possible that I am wrong?
and there is no greater meaning to life?
And things are this way – because…it is so.
For nothing is empty – void of substance
For within the universe of emptiness
There is divinity – the centerpiece of our being
The construct of order is conceptualization of space
Thoughts predicated on notion that 'I' is incomplete
For I am the only thing that seeks definitions
Truth predicated on truth mutes creative expression
Like fire marks the first stage of failure at the end
We simply start over to start again
What of the existential and The Prime Objective?
The deafening silence in the chamber of God
Must be the sound of ascending souls
Shush…listen carefully to the silence…
Can you hear your truth?

THE MESSAGE

These are the words:
"A dream
But not a dream
Tells of a stream
That runs blood
Turning the sea crimson red.
A flame,
but not a fire
That drains the spirit
And sucks the soul
Consuming the seed of good.
And as the sword cuts the rose
The victor - death cries, 'thirst!'
For victims are few
For all is void of life
In the day nature weeps, no more
And the Earth oozes molten hate
That singes the very thoughts of men.
And I wake…to smell the carnage.
As we turn the wheel
We wear the life of this - our home."
I have spoken.

I DREAM

I dream of love smothered in the depth of souls that can no longer sleep
….my lips are sealed.

I dream of nights that sparkle with sunshine
Of desert winds that blows mountains out to the sea

Of God - a rose in the eyes of a storm

Who hears the whispers in a garden?
When souls are dying constantly reaching out to be free.

I dream of sadness and the beauty
Of ancient desire and the search to be free
Of men like mice with innate contradictions
Who speaks of love as they place shackles here on my feet?

I dream of hearts that are too bold to surrender
Of restless arms that wait too long to caress
broken hearts that are sad but laden with valor
Who die in the memories of someone else's fight - so it seems?

I dream of hope but then I found wisdom
I dream of God - she stands reverently
I dream of words and behold - they have spoken
Things are never all that they seem – so I dream.

SIMPLICITY

A ray of light attracts a butterfly
-Whose feet were laced with pollen-
To venture to the other side of the rainbow
Where it is barren.

Light is the air that caresses
The notion that life is perpetual
And as pollen floats on tainted air
Above blood-soaked fields
Dreamers ponder surrealistic notions of a new day
Mutes forge better tomorrows from radioactive clay
Lepers twist neon lights into holographic paradigm.
Oblivious to descending pollen we seek to distort time

Overstated and magnified man simply failed to recognize
The singularity in God, the Cosmos, and the Light.
See, he never saw … The Butterfly.

THE BEGINNING

The sounds of darkness filled the room
as the broken glass
crunched under my naked feet…
I was not alone
and the smoke that blinded me eased
as the stench of the dead filled my nostrils
the people bowed to an open altar
and somewhere in the darkness
the drums that pounded my head
guided the beat of my heart
the lifeless body a Krist Child
faced-down in a pool of blood - rose
and pointed to a star
And the drums they roared
like The Beast
And the people – they rose from the ash
And danced to a strange silence
Then…then I noticed - I too, like they were -
dancing. dancing on broken glass
and the blood that flowed from our feet
created a stream
and **The Krist** Child beckoned to a star screaming:
"HAILE SELASSIE!" And scared the night
Then the glass changed to grass at my feet
Then all went quiet…
It was the Genesis - and **The Lion** roared!

CAN YOU FEEL LOVE?

One day...
You'll hear a song
And you'll feel warm inside
You'll drift back in time and remember...
You'll remember a poem
Hidden in a special place.
You will unfold a paper old
And slip fifty years in the past
And you will remember.
You'll remember him
You'll remember a time when you were
Afraid to love him
A time you doubted him
And open a world you had long forgotten
A world where sorrows were candy bars
And fear of mistakes was but dewdrops
Slipping off a leaf in some hidden garden.
For he created the words that made it so
...And so, it was.

For he shaped reality with a drinking straw
Leaving messages in the sands that reads:
"I love you"
He wrote poems of truth
That secretly swept your heart
He spoke about pumping love through eternity
And elevating photons, just for your love, saying:
"Can you feel it? - Can you feel it?
Oozing through your veins gushing, pulsating
Leaving you dazed- can you feel it?"
He was raw yet sensitive- tender yet strong
Poet, mathematician, revolutionary and writer of songs
He didn't give a heck about much
Was never afraid to touch...
He knew one thing for certain and that was:

Nothing lasts forever.
He knew that love was the greatest force
So, he loved completely, without fear
Without apprehension, without mercy,

without apology -without - question.
"Can you feel it,
shivering in your stomach when we embrace?"
Can you feel it echoing through eternity?
Basking in the foreverness of dreams unborn
Can you feel it? Can you feel it?"

He said:
Life's tragedy is a love unborn
Lest we capture moments true
We'll forever cherish yesterday's embrace.
So, he raved in the present for there lies true
Everything else is dreams or memories
They triumph only in the mind.

Now -time has slipped through the neck of an hourglass
And the twig that we planted - stands a great oak
A thousand seasons has worn mountains to plains
For as he said: nothing remains the same.

But a poem hidden in a secret place- open spaces and paused time
Faded old paper- traps eternity between lines.
Now children that once scamper in the hope of a new tomorrow -
Can't remember why...
But you'll remember fifty years ago
You'll remember
A poem, a song, a love.
A love that transcended time
A love that exists in melodies
A love encrypted in nursery rhymes
A voice saying:
"Can you feel it
Can you feel love?
Oozing through your veins –
like gushing, pulsating fire
Leaving you dazed.
Can you feel it? Can you feel it?"
And the wind will kiss your wrinkled cheeks
And chills will run up your spine like the first day
You read these words.
Can you feel it?
Can you feel it?
Tell me you can.

WARRIOR POETS

'Here! – Come with me'
Don't be mistaken by my appearance
Flared-leg blue jeans shaven clean with a low fade
Not the quintessential intellectual or the Messiah
I have no desire to be labeled
I do not care who rocked the cradle
But if I am not mistaken
It was dammed well shaken
Equally comfortable with a tech-nine or a pen
I've come again to walk amongst men
for they have sinned.
In times of old when I was cold
I would snatch heartbeats and open souls
No! …I do not seek to compete for favor
frivolity has no neighbors
I stood at the feet of God
and She told me about the light of salvation
She said to go and save your nation
with the fruits of your labor.
She told me to preach it - so now I teach it
Existing between modes she spoke of the Krist within me:

"Who else will bear the cross - but thee?"
Warrior poets have no friend but the sword they swing
Sword metamorphosed into, a guitar or a pen!
We scare souls on sight - Then we… scare them again!

Don't be shocked; there are no lines, no confines
So, by design I operate outside of the box
I'm a new-age Bob Marley without dreadlocks
I'm the essence of change a John Coltrain - just call me - Wayne
Brother you're right, you're right, you're right,
You're right, you're - so right
Scripting revolution in coded lyrics, rhythm, and notes -
I boast that I can float above all ills
I unfold reality at will
as I spill ink upon paper
and forge notes into sabers
Refusing to stand still for there're no reciprocities
Reciprocities in the philosophies of the fools

Who try to control me - Yo! - Nobody owns me
Dread! mi jussa move ahn thro'
(Hey! I'm just passing by)
To you I sing this strange song - don't get me wrong,
It won't be long before they enter my zone
Let it be known that I alone clone contempt.
Yet, time spent with me is never wasted or overstated
I exist in multiplicity - multiplicity
Living in the ghettoes of big cities - your city
It's a pity you think I am mere mortal - hmm
I bow down and ask forgiveness for your blasphemous ways - and
I -especially pray
For those who chose to stand in my way…
May their souls rest in peace - must
I repeat that as you dream schemes,
I observe the hyperbolic sine in naturally sagging lines you call catenaries
Those curves exist in the lips and the hips of my sisters who gave birth to
The Universe
And, for what it's worth - I claim we are the first to dance upon the
fragments of extinguishing stars.
I ice-skated upon the frozen tundra of Mars
Creating those scars, you call valleys.
I sling epithets to capture the vastness of Galaxies –
I ignore fallacies
I draft new-aged conjectures
between time space and reality
On off day's…I write Gangster rhyme
Using three syllables' words in hypothetical syllogisms
There are three eyes in the Prism…But let us - leave that alone
I set passive into motion, spit out verbs
like germs to cast doubts and scare lethargy
It's a pity you don't know me
But how can you control that which you don't know –
that which you can't own?
Were you not told of my Second Coming? –
Ah! - you never heard the drumming.
Yes! I am He – God - with a small 'g'.
 Nobody…told you - about me.
Well - my mother sent me here for thee
My momma said to set thee free.
Here! - Come with me.

INTANGIBLE

Time…
Rippling through the crevices of minds
Finds new beginning in laughter
Finds happiness in the fluttering of wings
There is no laughter here
The angels…they left yesterday

You are the essence of dreams unfolding
The fabric upon which humanity is etched
A tapestry- in its awakening
Dawned with rainbows, stars and all kinds of special things
And in my darkest hour I can hear your voice ring
I am at peace in your shadow
But…the clouds slip through my fingers
I am alone here-there is no shelter in this place

You- in your simplicity- are the template of creation
Sweet light air spruced with the fragrance of morning glory
The untold story of life and its revelations.
The unrehearsed steps of spirits dancing on morning dew
Casting shadows upon the moon
The sounds of nature slipping through canyons
Like the first arriving raindrops to kiss the desert floor
They sizzle upon contact-the ultimate sacrifice
Yet momentarily they bring earth to heaven

I do not know what to do
I do not know what to say
You're…so far away.

Is It I?

(Form poem)

The smoke swirls within the partly lit room of my mother's.
Is the chaos – I, or the essence of my emptiness?
I must confess that truth eludes me
Who am I…If I am not the agitator?
Is there any evidence of my wisdom?
I confess time bears no relevance to
me for as much as I am me…I'm also
we are therefore the keeper of sanity.
I am he who dwells in forgotten places
My body is the earth – andrioidigenos
The I in me is the core my spirituality
Without this I'm dust – ashes to ashes
My first thought is mere manifestation
of socialized protocols, perceived norms
My hyper-thoughts - subliminal poised
It dances within the darkness of dreams
I long to visit hyperspace past midnight
long to travel at the speed of black light
Let me stop - I might offend things hidden
But…speak I must: I've choreographed waltz
for mountains, now they dance while you are asleep
I compose sonatas in K-minor
Resonating in the realm of strings
Fiddled with dimensions -
I have an affinity for ten.
Hear my words propagated
In thoughtless weary minds
Who find solace in silent verses?
Verses captured in the incense that burns, that swirls
Swirling from a vase atop my mother's chest of drawers

LET IT BE

If I am to lose...
Let it be now
When I am strong
And have the strength to carry on.

If I must go...
Let me go now
Whilst the Sun shines
At least my way, I'll surely find.

If I must love...
Let it be now
When I can easily surrender
So I may rave in love's splendor.

If I must die...
Let it be...tomorrow
For I only just began to - live.

...Regarding the Quantum and Esoteric Realm

FUNTUNFUNEFU

Together we are blessed by our sheer multiplicity.
Guided by our faiths vilified by our audacity
The dreams that I have are not only for me
I hope that one day that all men will be free
When isolated we
Prey on adversities
But together we can find *UNITY in DIVERSITY.*

THE QUANTUM AND THE ESOTERIC REALM

(List Poem)

TRAVELERS [*we are searching*]
HEAR O LORD [*we have forgotten that*]
NOTHING IS ORDINARY [*unlike*]
THE CAGED CANARY [*we are driven by complexities*]
THE FIFTH ELEMENT [*has exposed our fragilities*]
SCARRED [*scared frightened*]
FOREVER YESTERDAY [*creeping? Screaming like*]

THE TRAVELER

Light restricts me by day so forgive me if my vision is marred

But by night I float between the fragments of extinguishing stars

Please forgive me –If I stumble for indeed, I've travelled far

I leaped through quasars and galaxies just to be where you are.

See I am a traveler in mourning…I am blessed, and I am cursed

I've seen hatred and sorrow and I don't know which one is the worst

The earth that gave us birth, now show us no mercy

Let me perch on your bench water bearer for I'm both tired and thirsty

And, if you offer me some water -I will speak the truth of my journey

For I've seen shape shifting-creatures in worlds constantly burning

Void of faith, hope and conviction - they had no celestial yearnings

Sent to proselytize a world, but conditions were worse than predicted

The people there were conflicted, vile, twisted, and even animalistic

They concoct their own truth; they claimed that honesty was overrated

And where there're no ethical precepts, morals soon become berated

The story I share with you now, I was not sent here to release

It is a soliloquy without ambit – both obscure and incomplete

Now, I will offer you a version of existence that is only yours to keep

Though I digress, for I contend that you might feel that you know me

We are the pious forms plying this road we are restless and lonely

We are on this endless trek to reclaim the savages' ancestral bones

We have lost our sainthood for we had left the heathens alone

So here we are on our penance, travelers of these ghastly zones

Only I and the carriers of water call these barren roads home

See, we're the characters of myths –known for our prowess and vigor

We are one in the same person – we need not look in the mirror

In truth, we are not certain which one of us arrived first

The seraph or the bearer all that we know is our thirst

As I crave your water, your one desire is to hear my mystical stories

Though I yearn for silence – I am not seeking fame or glory
Now that you have heard my tale, and it is true - I no longer thirst
I am at the end of my day, and we are both broken our cursed
Now point me to the hidden garden where the wretched children play
I must now collect the bones; and never repeat what I have said
Ah yes it was written – and I was meant to come here today
Now that I have rested my wings – push your cart out of my way.

HEAR O LORD
'Hear O lord the sound of my call...hear O lord and have mercy'.

I cannot sleep because it takes me to strange places that I know.

Places that I can't seem to remember if peaceful waters flow.

See, when souls ingest altered energies, they concoct their own creators.

Sending the grim reaper searching to find refuge in earthly manifestations.

I come here without fear, to comfort the discontented, the berated and the cursed.

See, we are meant to attract that which we are, but sometimes that is reversed.

So, I come here to share a little something about the things that make men thirst.

For we must turn our pain to wisdom, and we must turn night into day.

And despite being confident; sometimes...cynicism comes our way.

And those who brave this ghastly realm must learn to embrace moderation.

It was love that started this circle of life—it was love that sparked creation.

We do not harbor hatred, envy, or greed, nor should we ever seek for self.

We must imprint positive energy and imbue them in every moment spent.

Oftentimes, strengths conjure weaknesses, but love shines through it all.

Some will succumb to the scented candles that mask the stench that's down the hall.

While you don't fear me in person, you might fear the message I come to give.

For you know we cannot be ambivalent —-about the life we chose to live.

See, sages, dreamers, and discerners — they all have pre-ordained missions.

So, when paths do not align with callings —prayers can't come to full fruition.

It's not that your prayers are not answered, it could be that you are not learning.

See, the universe is energy in motion and emotes its own elevated yearnings.

When you walk your path, you'll float unincumbered in the unholiest of spaces.

Your vibration speaks to who you are – and opens doors in hidden hollow places.

So, I came back here, in the event, that you are still trying to find your way.

To share these uncommon words with you – as it came plainly to me today.

You need to shed all earthly distractions the next time you kneel to pray.

See…you know that you are anointed; but first, you must proudly claim your gift.

Furthermore, you should not be the epicenter of the things you seek to uplift.

And, if truth be told, there is even greater solace in seeking just the opposite.

So, you should pray for humanity and hope that they somehow find their way.

Remember to pray for a sacred garden where the children can safely play.

Pray for those who have fallen and for those who have lost their merit.

Don't forget to pray for the meek, the simple and for the earth, they shall inherit.

And, that being said…and for what it's worth—send this prayer into the universe.

And it will reverberate in multiplicity giving you the things you most deserve.

And in closing these verses, I would like to suggest just one more simple thing.

Reread the poem I sent last week – about the canary and why it sings.

'My soul is longing for the glory of you…so hear O lord and answer me'.

NOTHING IS ORDINARY

A casual walk can help us find some momentary peace.

And we might find a basking angel in someone that we meet.

Perhaps – today will be gentle—less routine and less predictable.

There is nothing less celebrated than that which is made simple.

It is quite possible that today will help you break the monotony.

For there might be a chance 'hello' that might offer us some clarity?

See, no one ever warned us that life could suck up all our energies.

How it can turn good friends into foes and lovers into enemies

For, once scampering feet – make their retreat... And even blur our vision of the very things we seek.

For the winds of change may come our way and knock us off our feet.

And that stranger peering back in the mirror - is somehow really me.

There are no proclamations or announcements the wheel of life just simply spins.

And it just might be a chance encounter that alter what it brings.

For today cannot be yesterday as much as the absence of love cannot be seen as hatred.

And without grounding and affirmation, we might be left exposed or even naked.

There is no mercy for our inactions – it's not like a dream deferred.

There are countless opportunities loss in words spoken but never heard.

So, we package our broken promises into little brown paper bags.

Still fussing, in our silence, about the things we never had.

Sacrificed, compromising in this ever-spinning wheel.

Trying to understand our nature and the way we truly feel.

And we still wake up tired from our long-forgotten dreams.

Not remembering their details and never knowing what they mean.

We move from chasing tiny promises and slapping little-tiny hands.

Now they have all grown into strangers – that we don't seem to understand.

Soon, there are things we can't remember – and that had always been our fear.

And it's strange we never noticed the changing colors of our hair.

For all, we have come to treasure, for all that we have planned.

All our celebrated moments all our achievements -small and grand.

In time, they will all just simply fade away like wet footprints in the sand

So, learn to embrace all your moments, and learn to celebrate your nows.

For, life is forever fleeting, and soon old friends won't be around.

To remember past time cherished, and to call us by our names.

For we are truly never certain that tomorrow will come our way.

So, nothing is ordinary…so take the time to say hello.

For, we can't tell who is saint, or sinner; so go ahead and take a chance.

For it is hard for one to spot an angel on a momentary glance.

WHY THE CAGED CANARY SINGS?

It's fair to say that we have encountered souls that have never seen the light.

Just like the canary in an open cage, that has never taken flight.

There're unknowns regarding things we know --now if that's too hard to manage.

Well... imagine the things unknown, about things we don't know – that's even harder to imagine.

See, the caged canary sings, atop its wire-gilded throne.

It sings without reservation or complaints -and it often sings alone.

And if we truly to understand the reason why it sings.

We might come to understand the void that lives within us still.

We are confused with the notion of the space and time divides.

And the breadth of our expanded sphere it's still left undefined.

Growth means the extension of one's experiences or one's intellectual span.

It must be entailed organizing schemas and processes to make us better understand.

What of our invisible selves, or the unexplored mind as the center of our being?

What of purpose, or of salvation, and the things that are unseen?

So, we envision the caged canary's universe as a sparsely unlit room.

It seems, the canary never sees the outside world, and that's what we've assumed.

We think the canary acquiesces to a banal world —forever locked.

We see the bird's eternity trapped within a quaint ignoble box.

See, it is easy for us to worry about a life confined or void of regal plurality.

A life trapped within a confined space – is antithetical to our perceived humanity.

For, for all we know, the bird should be defiant, for its imprisoned in a cage.

But the canary simply hops from perch to branch, it sings, and yes ...it plays.

But there are human souls just like our canary, they flutter in unlit confines.

But unknown to them is the canary's conception of value, space, and time.

See...a soul that surrenders its own freedom to someone else's scheme.

Will, in a moment, acquiesce to the whim or fervor of someone else's dreams.

They will never experience the contentment, gained when one is driven by their own spirit.

Unlike us, the canary...it never tires for It is not restrained by fabricated limits.

See, the canary —It cares nothing about, the sounds of the distant beating drums.

It's unincumbered, and unperturbed by the thought, that tomorrow may or may not come.

The canary remains determined, for it is driven by its own celestial wisdom.

It cannot be constrained by compulsions that derived from fable paper kingdom.

So, all that we are and without question, all that we can ever be.

Are grounded and constrained by our altered perceptions and our sense of reality.

So, our notion of truth, and our conception of time are relative – so I am asking you to stop!

As it is now abundantly clear that we are -at best- enslaved by our clocks.

See, we are mesmerized by shiny objects... anchored to the earthly things we got.

So, for all we know the canary sings to guide us, it sings to ease our pain.

It sings because we are wounded souls, and it wants to help us find our way.

It sings for eternal simplicity – if not now...then maybe before the end of day.

It hopes that we would find our wings and take off in the night.

It hopes that we might defy all logics and take that inner flight.

But we are unaware of our enslavement, we never noticed our own cage.

Never, in all our wisdom, realize the very life we live is staged.

So, the bird it tries to comfort us – now... isn't that something?

With all of God's great glory and with its broken, tattered wings.

The canary seeks to comfort us...and that is why —it sings.

THE FIFTH ELEMENT (SPECIAL ED.).

The gifted eyes sense things before its conception before it becomes real.

It might be their heightened awareness in areas, that by design, we simply can't conceive.

It might be a kaleidoscopic milieu of motions that dwells beyond our clarity.

Maybe, it's a subterranean tunnel, in a vortex, that is sustains its own microgravity.

It might be a multidimensional plain, connected by swinging interlocking patterns.

In a realm beyond our comprehension one that is not governed by what we know as matter.

But there are those who sense fears, see the outlines of feigns, and pain in its awakening.

They can account for something in its birth and digest emotions before they are created.

But can you model congealed sensations at the edge of a quasi-time-space continuum?

But time begets urgency, so that conception is beyond your conventional wisdom.

But can you bend light into colors and mold words into pictural representations?

And do this pristine judgement void of without anglicized bastardization?

Can one craft the term 'gifted' when minds are shaped by the realities they meet?

And our understanding of consciousness is, at best, incomplete?

What do you call someone who can see word vibrating, or feel the color trapped in the light?

Or taste the sounds of falling angels as they scamper through the tainted air at night?

There are things unexplored or, ignored that contradict your story of Nativity.

There are no instructions to teach vision, nor a scale to measure a child's creativity.

See, education is political, it is not inclusive, but we are forced to work with it.

Now, here is a littler exercise, and it is not designed to determine your intellect or wit.

Now, imagine a piper paying in a five-dimension garden, in a realm that far away.

Project the piper's image on yonder wall - now...can you see the music she plays?

To visualize sound in the 5th dimension is a task that's well beyond our grasp.

It takes imagination and even acculturation, to address the very questions that we ask.

See multiculturism, cannot be viewed from through a prism -we are from different worlds.

And in the aforementioned test; did you envisioned the piper as a girl?

For, we are restrained by the medium we have created and imprisoned by our labors.

Diluted truth can be induced, but it will not produce new fruits, new shoots nor flavors.

So, whether educated or schooled academic offerings are often too robust far too structured.

So, send this poem of descent to the hooded keepers atop your ivory towered clusters.

Can you titillate one's sense of feel and bring light to things yet created?

See, creative impulses cannot be confined to boxes locked into little, tiny spaces.

So, what is 'special education 'or 'gifted', I urge you to answer this call to duty.

I am denouncing your odium precepts that separate the gifted from the unruly.

Some may call this insurrection, and few might come to offer aid.

All our kids are special, and you just do not know...how geniuses are made.

SCARRED

The heart seldom knows it is broken. Sometimes…the search outside reflects the void within

For often, our deepest wounds they never break the surface of the skin.

Functionally depressed, we digress and cast our nets into the ocean.

Attempting frantically to dissipate any latent emotions.

For feelings are uncanny, they can rupture our façade.

We may never know we are broken – so we never gather up our shards.

But I am here to show you mine if you dare to show me yours.

Sometimes it is easy to surrender, easier still to just ignore

See…it's hard to open the very door —the one that led you to despair.

Thinking no one really got our backs, and maybe no one really cares.

Surely no one will come along and pause to truly listen to a story.

One that's unflattering, demeaning, and not clamoring for glory

So, it's easier to sit, it's hard to open-up, and even harder to commit It's challenging to face our fears — and it's easier to quit.

For we've learned to never break our cycle; to stay composed and occupied

Surely, no one will know we are vulnerable - if we don't let them come inside.

So, we stay true, quiet, and innocuous --for we are truly who we are.

Acquiescing, condescending, but forever deeply scarred.

See…the heart…seldom knows... it's broken, without a cogent search within

For the deepest wounds —sometimes never break the surface of the skin.

FOREVER YESTERDAY

Gentle are the winds that blow
To remove the veil off things less known.
We cry because we know the cost
Of friends who are forever lost
And we too will come to close our eyes
As we one day come to realize
We're simply the thoughts that we create
Combined with the emotions we radiate
Many will choose to come and play
And fewer still will come to stay
I'll never question why you leave your posts.
If I am the one you love the most
For we're merely passing vessels upon life's raging seas

And what will be— will surely be
So, reflect on your actions, and analyze your past
While the tides are high, they too won't last
Sometimes it hard to rectify
Still the truth we fear we cannot hide
So, if by chance you care to grow
To escape the cycle, you've come to know
It was your call that brought me here
And yes, I know you're not prepared
For soon the wheels will spin again
Its unannounced, its beginnings and ends
And...soon someone will come your way…
But for us it's forever… Yesterday.

NYAME DUA

I

My mark is not a rose...not a clover...nor a flower.
Angels carrying savage weapons.
Gathered at the base of a broken crucifix–
Eyes affixed, lay waiting...whispering.
Light seeps through stained glass and down a spiral staircase
Which leads to a darkened chamber...where no shadows fall...
But feathers do...like snowflakes or scented morning dew
For angels - they whiz above ... like albatrosses or white-breasted doves.
I do not know what brought me here... Is this the sum of all my fears?
I knew of all the sins I bore, and promises...I had ignored.
And as angels chattered up above...
Why do I understand their tongue?
I do have sins...that I must face,
Did it lead me to this ghastly place?
Could it be that these are my final hours?
My mark is not a rose...not a clover...nor a flower.

II

For I knew then that it was not right
When I shed, my skin and I took flight.
To wage a war upon the hooded claws
That casted their shadows on her walls
For I have strangled gargoyles whilst she sleeps
So that she could have her visions and dream her dreams.
I knew it was wrong, but I had to rush
Now — who shall take from me this cup?
Now as I pondered on these things.
I noticed that I too —- had wings
Who placed within my hand this saber?

For I have not toiled, nor truly labored.

I have only dried the tears she cried, and sang to her a lullaby

Dreams had taught me how to rhyme, and search for cryptic mystic signs.

I know of many who have suffered long... I must make the point — there is something wrong.

I will argue that someone erred...

For, I know nothing of scriptures, nor sacred words.

I have only offered her a shoulder to lean on and, in the depth of her nights...I wrestled her demons.

I knew the war they claimed was coming.

Was upon us - for I had heard the drumming

Saw the Heathens running - knew soon, days will be over.

My mark is not a flower, not a rose…nor a clover.

III

Then SHE spoke to me without speaking….

Like in a dream but without the dreaming.

She said: **Who then will paint the doors with lamb's blood?**

And etch on their skin the sacred seals.

Who will clean the –soot off the Messiahs?

And tell them of a world -- lit only by fires.

Who will write these coded words on parchment paper...

Then pommel evil spirits later?

And who will know these things are true?

Some have a single pair of wings —my son…

But you have two!

But I'm just a soldier, a writer, a lowly dreamer.

I know nothing about the true redeemer.

My son FEAR NOT ...do as you are told!!

Your mark is not a flower, nor a clover nor a rose.

IV

The light dances with the shadows - beneath darkened staircase

And as angels and warrior poets repair to their sacred chambers.

To wage war - we all know well.

We prepare, again, to raise Cain upon the gates of hell.

To make sure hell's gates are forever sure, and tight

We patrol the margins between darkness and light.

So, the world, may safely go to sleep.

And restless kids, can count their sheep.

We do not fight for fame or favors.

We know that death has thirteen flavors.

We have faced them all -- a thousand times.

But we've pledge to make that sacrifice.

See…the light that starts a brand-new day, will wash our memories… all away

But tomorrow's night will fall again, and between the tics of time – relent.

Again, we will unfold our wings, and we'll grab our sabers.

And again, we'll enter these darkened chambers.

See, by day, we know not what we are; but by night, through love, we travel far

Above blood-soaked field, through fiery realms, known only to demons, sages, and sentinels.

Our wounds, they leave, these battle scars.

They are our trophies — they are our vailed cryptic scars.

Still…I dare not speak of things yet told…

My mark is not a flower, nor a clover…nor a rose.

A PRAYER

Mother Earth --I come before you…l am—broken, tired and spent

Father God— the universe sends me words that just ooze —from my pen

Some of these messages I can decipher; but others —I can't comprehend.

Lord...I'm here as your loyal servant and, on me...you can depend

Lord…I am trying to stay patient, upright and just… do as I 'm told

But it seems like nights are getting darker and the vipers –now they're bold.

I've sent your notes to the angels --sometimes...I write through the night.

But lately...my quill is getting mightily heavy and my sword—invitingly light.

Could it be that there's a breach in the wall – that we have sworn to protect?

And the lines are already broken -- I'm just trying to be — circumspect.

Lord...you know I've had some issues, in the past, with...following your rules.

Well—perhaps more than a little issue…to tell the honest-truth.

But I find days are getting shorter-- and souls are getting enraged and agitated.

Lord, you have given me this gift, and now I know —what my true name is!

Forgive me...for I'm shouting – and yes...it's true, there's still much to write.

But...Lord...as I am dropping your verses – Please...permit me to fight.

For there are shapeless forms seeking to lay prey upon our angels in waiting.

They have no spiritual signature – and Lord I swear —I'm not mistaken.

I gave the angels the decree you sent me, now she can detect the hooded liars.

She will see those oblivious to the written truth – and those seeking to conspire.

For, there are vultures who crawl out of dark places void of grace or authentic desires.

I am restricted by my celestial vows– so I can only speak— as is required.

These words will not clean the soot off the Messiah; they're not meant to inspire.

They were meant to expose the traps or snares set by serpents and submerged pariahs.

My Lord If the walls are already breached and there're creatures — roaming the streets.

Please...I beg you Father ...call me by name—I place my swords at your feet.

And if, by chance, other sentinels should come to make the same claims or inquire.

Lord...my armor is here. should I tell them of that morbid place…... as the text requires?

I come before you Father God— in praise, but more so in prayer.

Now...is it time to speak of a dark, gruesome world?

A world…lit only…by fires.